Books by
Edith M. Patch

NATURE STUDY
Dame Bug and Her Babies

Hexapod Stories

Bird Stories

First Lessons in Nature Study

Holiday Pond

Holiday Meadow

Holiday Hill

Holiday Shore

Mountain Neighbors

Desert Neighbors

Forest Neighbors

Prairie Neighbors

NATURE AND SCIENCE READERS
Hunting

Outdoor Visits

Surprises

Through Four Seasons

Science at Home

The Work of Scientists

HUNTING

HUNTING

by

Edith M. Patch
and Harrison E. Howe

illustrated by

Eleanor Osborn Eadie

YESTERDAY'S CLASSICS

ITHACA, NEW YORK

This edition, first published in 2022 by Yesterday's Classics, an imprint of Yesterday's Classics, LLC, is an unabridged republication of the text originally published by the Macmillan Company in 1932. For the complete listing of the books that are published by Yesterday's Classics, please visit www.yesterdaysclassics.com. Yesterday's Classics is the publishing arm of Gateway to the Classics which presents the complete text of hundreds of classic books for children at www.gatewaytotheclassics.com.

ISBN: 978-1-63334-185-2

Yesterday's Classics, LLC
PO Box 339
Ithaca, NY 14851

GAMES IN THIS BOOK

Part One—*Hunting for Holes*

Part Two—*Hunting in the School Garden*

Part Three—*Hunting in the Park*

Part Four—*Hunting in the Zoo*

PART ONE

Hunting for Holes

Ted's Hole

Ted dug a hole.
He dug the hole with a spade.

Ann came to see Ted's hole.
"Ann, see my hole," said Ted.
Ann said, "It is a big hole."

A Good Game

Uncle Jim came to see Ted's
  hole.
He said, "It is a big hole.
To-day I saw some little holes."

Ted said, "We will hunt and
  find the little holes."

Ann said, "It will be a good
  game."

The Ant Hole

Ann found a hole.
It was a little hole.
Some ants dug the hole.
Some ants ran into the hole.
Some ants ran out of the hole.

Each ant had six legs.
Each ant had two feelers
   on its head.
Each ant waved its feelers.

The Mole Hole

Ted found a hole.
It was a little hole.
Moles dug it with their hands.
The moles were blind.
They could dig without seeing.

The blind moles had fur.
Their fur was soft and warm.
Blind Father Mole was a
    hunter.
Mother Mole was a hunter,
    too.
They hunted for food.
They hunted in their holes.
They could hunt without
    seeing.

The moles had a nest.
Their nest was in the hole.
Four baby moles were in the
    nest.
The four baby moles were
    blind.
Blind Mother Mole took good
    care of the baby moles.
She could do it without
    seeing.

The Swallow Hole

Two birds dug a hole in a
  bank.
They dug it with their bills.
One bird was Father Bank
  Swallow.
One bird was Mother Bank
  Swallow.
They were brown and white.

The birds made a nest in the
hole.
Mother Bank Swallow laid four
eggs in the nest.
She kept the four eggs warm.

A baby bird grew in each egg.
Each bird grew and filled the
shell.
The shell broke and the bird
hatched.

Father and Mother Bank Swallow
hunted for flies.
They gave flies to the baby birds
in the nest.
The baby birds could not hunt
for their flies.
Father and Mother Bank Swallow
took good care of them.

One day Ted and Ann found
the hole.

They saw Father Bank Swallow
hunt.

He took some flies in his bill.

He took them into the hole.

Ted said, "He is a good
hunter."

"He is a pretty bird," said Ann.

The Squirrel Hole

Ted and Ann saw a hole in a
    tree.
Mother Squirrel ran into the
    hole.
The squirrel had gray fur
    and a big gray tail.
Ted and Ann liked to see her.

Ted put a peanut near the tree.
He and Ann sat on the
    ground and they were very
    quiet.

The squirrel came out of the
    hole.
She ran down the tree and
    found the peanut.

Mother Squirrel made a nest
and Father Squirrel helped
her.
It was in the top of a tree.
It was made with dry leaves.
Four baby squirrels lived in it.
They were not old enough to
climb.
Mother Squirrel took care of
them.

The Woodpecker Hole

Ted and Ann found a hole in
   a tree.
The tree was old and had no
   leaves.

Ted said, "I will climb this
   tree."

"I will climb it, too," said Ann.

Ted said, "Perhaps a squirrel
    lives in this hole!
    Perhaps a bird lives in it!
    Shall we sit near a bush
    and watch the hole?"

They sat near a bush and were
    quiet.

Two pretty birds flew to the
    tree.
One bird was black and white.
She was Mother Woodpecker.
One was black and white and
    red.
He was Father Woodpecker.
The back of his head was red.
The two birds climbed the tree
    and dug little holes in it.
They found food with their
    bills.

The woodpeckers had a nest
in the hole in the old tree.
Five white eggs were in the
nest.
Mother Woodpecker laid them
there.
She took good care of her eggs.
She sat on them to warm them.
All the eggs needed to be
warm.
A baby bird grew in each egg.

It grew too big for its shell.
So it broke the shell and
hatched.

All the young birds were
hungry.
They could not climb or fly.
Their father and mother fed
them.
They ate and grew big and
their feathers grew, too.
They grew old enough to fly
and climb and pick for food.

Ted and Ann saw them come
out and pick little holes in
the tree.
They ran to tell Uncle Jim,
"We saw five young
woodpeckers with black and
white feathers."

The Cricket Hole

A little black cricket had a
  home in a hole in the
  ground.
He had six legs and he could
  run.
He had wings on his back,
  but he could not fly with
  them.
He made a happy sound with
  them.
The sound was like, "Cree-cree!"

Ted and Ann found the cricket
 hole.
They sat on the ground to
 watch it.
They were quiet while they
 watched.

Little black Father Cricket
 came out of his hole in the
 ground.
His two feelers waved and
 waved.
Two of his wings made no
 sound.
His two top wings went,
 "Cree-cree!"

Mother Cricket came to hear
 him.
Her two feelers waved and
 waved.

She had six legs and she
   could run.
She had wings on her back,
   too.
She could not fly with them
   or make a happy sound
   with them.
She liked to hear Father
   Cricket.
Black Mother Cricket made a
   hole.

She laid her eggs in the hole.
She did not sit on her little
  eggs.
They were in the ground all
  winter.
The ground was very cold in
  winter.
There were baby crickets in
  the eggs but they were too
  cold to hatch.

But the ground was warm in
  spring!
So the eggs were warm in
  spring!
The warm baby crickets
  hatched.
They all came out of the
  ground.

They had feelers and waved
    them.

They had legs and ran with
    them.

But they had no wings at all.

The young crickets ate and
    grew.

Wings grew on their backs.

At first their wings were little.

The crickets ate more and grew
  more.
At last they were as big
  as Father and Mother
  Cricket.
And their wings were as big
  as the wings of old crickets.
Then they were grown crickets.

The sister crickets had quiet
  wings like the wings of
  Mother Cricket.
But the brother crickets had
  wings like the wings of
  Father Cricket.
So the brothers made a glad
  sound.
The sound was like,
  "Cree-cree!"

The Woodchuck Hole

Father Woodchuck dug a hole
and Mother Woodchuck
helped him.
The hole was their home.
There was a nest in the hole.
The nest was made of dry
grass.
Baby woodchucks were in the
nest.

Mother Woodchuck fed them
   milk.
The milk was good for them.

They could not run and play
while they were very young.
They could drink milk and grow.

When they were old enough
   to run, they played in the
   sunshine.
The sunshine was good for
   them.

They could sit on their hind
   legs.
They could use their paws for
   hands.

The woodchucks could not say
   words, but they could whistle.
That was the way they talked.

One day Ted and Ann hunted
and found the woodchuck hole.

They sat near it and did not
talk. They were quiet while
they watched.

Six young woodchucks came out
and played in the sunshine.
Ted and Ann often went to see
the six young woodchucks
play.

They liked to watch them
    eat flowers and leaves.
They liked to hear them whistle.

One day Ann had some candy
    in her hand.
Her hand was on the ground.
One woodchuck found the
    candy.
He took the candy and held it
    in his little paws and ate it.

Ted and Ann laughed when they
    saw the woodchuck eat the
    candy.
The woodchucks all ran to the
    hole when Ted and Ann
    laughed!

The Bumblebee Hole

A bumblebee hunted for a hole.
She needed a hole for her
home.
The bumblebee hummed with her
wings while she hunted for a
home.
The humming was like a song.
At last the bumblebee found a
hole.

The hole was in a mouse nest.
It was an old nest.
The mouse had moved out of it.

The bumblebee liked the old
nest and she moved into it.
Then she had a very good home.

The bumblebee made some bee
bread.
She made it with honey and
pollen.

She found nectar in some
flowers.
The nectar was like sweet water.
She changed the nectar to
honey.

She found pollen in flowers, too.
It was like pretty yellow dust.

Mother Bumblebee laid some
 eggs.
A baby bumblebee was in each
 egg.
The baby bees hatched.
They had no legs or wings.
They had no black or yellow
 hairs.
The baby bees liked the bee
 bread.
They ate it and grew fat.

The fat baby bees went to sleep.
They rested in their cocoons.

Each bumblebee waked and
came out of her cocoon.
She was not a baby bee then.
She had six legs and four
wings.
She had black and yellow hairs.
She was a grown bumblebee
when she came out of her
cocoon.

The grown bumblebees flew to
flowers for pollen and sweet
nectar.
They hummed with their wings
when they flew to the
flowers.
The humming was like a song.

Ted and Ann saw the bumblebee
hole.

The bumblebees saw Ted and
Ann.

Their buzzing was a cross
sound.

Ted and Ann ran to tell Uncle
Jim, "The bees were cross and
buzzed!"

He said, "They will sting you
if you go too near their hole.
They take care of their home."

Uncle Jim said, "You may watch bees when they are in flowers."

So Ted and Ann went to a rose bush.
They were very quiet and the bumblebees did not sting them.

The bees took pollen from the rose and hummed with their wings.
The humming was like a happy song.

Where and How?

How did Ted dig his hole?

Where were the feelers of the ants?

How did the moles dig their hole?
Where did the baby moles live?

Where do bank swallows dig holes?
How do they dig their holes?
Where do the baby swallows live?
How do swallows find food?

Where was the squirrel hole Ted and Ann found?
Where did the squirrels put their dry leaves?

Word Game

Where will you put each word?

climb   ground   whistle   hole
food   peanut   wings   milk

Ted and Ann could ____.
Ted gave the squirrel a ____.
The woodpecker nest was
   in a ____.
Father Cricket made a happy
   sound with two of his ____.
The cricket eggs were in the

   ____.
The two old swallows gave flies
   to their young for ____.
The baby woodchucks
   drank ____.
The woodchucks could ____.

If I Find a Hole

If I find a hole
   Down in the ground,
I'll keep still
   And not make a sound!

I'll watch for moles
   And woodchucks, too.
If you find a hole,
   What will you do?

If you find a hole
   Up in a tree,
Will you keep still
   As you can be?

PART TWO

Hunting in the
School Garden

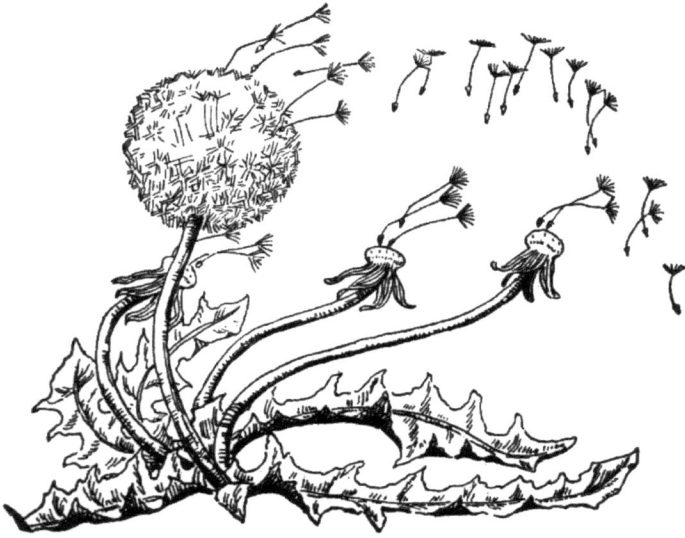

The School Garden

Ted and Ann went to school.
Their teacher was Miss Bell.
They told Miss Bell about
  hunting.

"We played a game," said Ann.

"The game was Hunting for
  Holes," said Ted.

Miss Bell smiled and said,
"That was a very good game.
Do you wish to play a new
game?"

"What is the new game?" asked
Ted.

Miss Bell said, "You may call
it Hunting in the School
Garden."

"May we hunt to-day?" asked
Ann.

"Yes, you may," said their teacher.

"How shall we hunt?" asked Ted.

Then Miss Bell told them,
"Hunt for plants and animals.
You may find an animal that
hops.
You may find one that flies."

The Sleepy Toad

A man was digging
    in the school garden.

"Why do you dig?" asked Ted.

"The ground is hard," said the
    man. "Most plants need soft
    ground."

The man dug up some more
soil.
He dug up a toad, too!
The toad did not hop or move.
It did not open its eyes.

"What a quiet toad!" said Ted.

"Is the toad sleepy?" asked Ann.

"Yes," said the man, "put it
in the sunshine and watch it.
Toads sleep in the winter
while they are cold.
They wake in the warm
spring."

Ted put the toad in the
sunshine.
He watched it open its eyes.
At last it hopped.

Ted took the toad in his hands.
He showed it to Miss Bell.

"Shall we give it food?" asked
Ann.

"No," said Miss Bell, "please
put it near the pond in the
park.
It will be glad to find water."

"Do toads go to ponds?" asked Ted, "Do they go to water like frogs?"

Miss Bell said, "Toads live on land and they live in water, too. In spring they go to water. They sit in the water and sing. Toads lay their eggs in water. Baby tadpoles hatch from the eggs. Tadpoles grow to be toads."

Ann asked, "May we keep tadpoles in school when they hatch?"

"Yes," said Miss Bell, "if you will take good care of them."

So they took the toad to the pond.

Little Red Trumpets

A plant grew in the school
   garden.
It was about six years old.
Its roots were in the ground.
Its stems climbed up a tree.
It had no leaves in winter.

The plant had new leaves in
spring.

It had flowers in spring, too.

The flowers were red and
yellow.

They were long like little
trumpets.

Ted asked Miss Bell about the
flowers in the school garden.

He said, "Have they any
nectar?"

She said, "Yes, they have nectar
and it is like sweet water."

"The flowers are long," said Ted.
"What can get the nectar?"

Miss Bell smiled and said,
"Watch the flowers some day
and perhaps you will see!"

Hummingbirds

Two birds came to the red
flowers.

They were very, very little,
but they had long bills.

The birds put their long bills
into the flowers to take
nectar.

Ted and Ann watched the two
birds.

Eleanor Osborn Eadie

They were quiet while they
watched.
Ted and Ann could hear the
humming sound of the wings.

One bird was Father
Hummingbird and one was
Mother Hummingbird.

Father Hummingbird had a
green back and a red throat.
Mother Hummingbird had
a green back and a white
throat.

Ted and Ann ran to tell Miss
Bell.
Ann said, "We saw some little
birds with humming wings.
They put their long bills
into the red trumpets for
nectar!"

Forget-me-not

One day Miss Bell asked,
    "Who hunted in the garden
    to-day?"

"Ann and I hunted to-day," said
    Ted, "and we found a pretty
    plant."

"It had pink buds," said Ann,
    and its flowers were blue."

Miss Bell said, "Please cut a
stem for each boy and girl."

Ted cut the stems and then
each boy and girl took one.

Miss Bell said, "There are no
roots on the stems Ted cut
for you. But there are leaves
and flowers. Watch the stems
each day."

Miss Bell filled a glass with
water. Then she said, "Each
boy and girl may put a stem
into this glass."

The boys and girls put the
stems into the glass and
watched them.

One day Ann said, "See the
stems in the glass of water!
There are white roots on
them!"

"The stems are plants now
    with roots," said Ted.

The boys and girls took the
    stems into the school
    garden.
They put the stems into wet
    ground and put soil on the
    new roots.

So each boy and girl had a
    plant.
Its name was forget-me-not.

A Weed

A plant grew in the school
 garden.
Its name was dandelion.
Its leaves were near the
 ground.
The dandelion flowers were
 yellow.
They grew on the tops of long
 stems.

One day the boys and girls went into the school garden. They saw the dandelion plant.

A girl said, "Dandelions are weeds. We do not let them grow at home."

A boy said, "They are good to eat. I dig dandelions each spring. Mother cooks the young plants."

Ted asked, "What is a weed?"

Miss Bell said, "A weed is a plant that people do not like to have. Dandelions are often weeds. They are weeds when they grow where people wish other plants."

Seeds grew on the flower
stems.

Then the long dandelion stems
had pretty white heads.

The boys and girls liked to
play with the white seed
heads.

They watched the little seeds.

The seeds went away with the
wind.

The Red Lily

Uncle Jim gave Ted a bulb
and he gave Ann some
seeds.

Uncle Jim said, "I found the
bulb and I found the seeds.
They grew on a lily plant."

Ted showed his bulb to Miss
Bell.
She said, "You may put it in
the school garden."

So Ted dug a hole in the
ground and put his bulb
into it.
Then he put some soil on the
bulb.

The bulb rested in the ground.
It rested all the cold winter
days.

The ground was warm in spring.
So the bulb was warm then, too.
The warm bulb grew in the
    sunshine.
A stem grew up from the bulb.
There were long leaves on the
    stem.

Ted hunted for his plant in
    spring.
He found it in the sunshine.
He told Miss Bell about it.
"The lily has a stem with leaves
    but it has no flowers," he said.

Miss Bell said, "You may hunt
    in the school garden this
    summer. You and Ann may
    watch the lily. Perhaps you
    will find a flower if you hunt
    for it in summer."

Ted's lily had flowers in summer.
Ted went to the garden to see
them.
Ann went with him.
The flowers were red and brown.
There was brown pollen in
them.
Some little bees came for pollen.
Ted and Ann watched the bees.

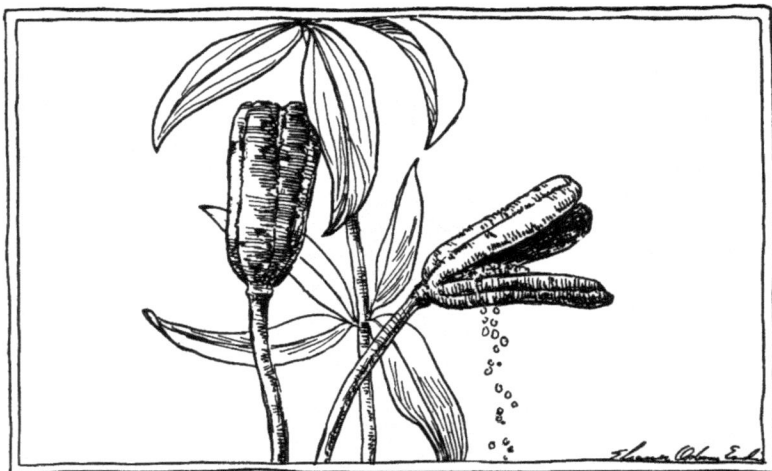

Ann told Miss Bell about the
  seeds that Uncle Jim gave
  her.
Miss Bell said,
  "You may plant them
  in the school garden."

So Ann put the seeds in the
  garden.
The lily seeds rested all winter.

Ann hunted for her lily plants when summer came.

Then she told Uncle Jim about them.

"Ted's lily is a big one," she said, "but my lily plants are little. They have little bulbs and stems."

He said, "Your plants are too young to have flowers this year."

"When will they be old enough to have flowers?" asked Ann.

"When they are four years old," said her uncle. "Then they will have big bulbs like the bulb I gave to Ted."

What Is It?

Toads go to it in spring.
Mother Toad puts her eggs in
   it.
The baby toads live in it.
What is it?

It is sweet like water.
Bumblebees find it in flowers.
Hummingbirds drink it.
What is it?

It has a bulb in the ground.
It has long green leaves.
It has red and brown flowers.
What is it?

Word Game

How will you use each word?

pink   nectar   green   weeds
blue   winter   throat   wind

The forget-me-not flowers are
   ___.
The forget-me-not buds are ____.
The dandelion seeds went away
   with the ____.
Father Hummingbird had a red
   ___.
His back was ____.
Hummingbirds put their long
   bills into long flowers for ____.
The toad was sleepy in ____.
People do not like some plants
   and they call them ____.

If I Find a Flower

If I find a flower,
    I'll watch to see
If a hummingbird comes
    And a bumblebee!

There is nectar sweet
    In a flower cup.
I'll watch to see
    If they drink it up!

If you find a flower,
    Will you watch to see
If a hummingbird comes
    And a bumblebee?

PART THREE

Hunting in the Park

The Park

A man took good care of the
    park.
His name was Mr. Long.
He told Ted and Ann about
    plants.
He told them about animals,
    too.
Mr. Long was their kind friend.

"The biggest plants in the park are the trees," said Mr. Long.

"May we help you take care of the trees?" asked Ted.

"You may help me when I cut off old dry branches," said Mr. Long.

"Some of the animals in the park have fur," said Mr. Long.

"Squirrels have fur," said Ann. "We will help take care of them."

So Ted and Ann gave peanuts to the squirrels in the park.

"Some of the animals in the park have feathers," said Mr. Long.

"Birds have feathers," said Ted. "Uncle Jim gave us a box for the birds. Will you put it up on a tree?"

"Yes," said Mr. Long, "I will."

Father and Mother Bluebird
came and made a nest in the
box.
They made it with brown dry
grass.

Mother Bluebird liked to hear
Father Bluebird sing his songs.

There were four pretty blue eggs
in the bluebird nest.
Mother Bluebird kept them
warm.

When the four young birds
hatched they were hungry.
They all opened their mouths.

So their father and mother
hunted.
The old birds found food for
the hungry young bluebirds.

One day Ted and Ann told Mr. Long about their hunting games.

"We played one game," said Ann. "Its name was Hunting for Holes.

"The other game we played," said Ted, "was Hunting in the School Garden."

Mr. Long smiled and asked them, "Do you wish to play a new game? You may call it Hunting in the Park."

Ted said, "That is a good game, too!"

"We will hunt to-day," said Ann. So Ted and Ann went hunting.

Toads and Tadpoles

One spring day Ted and Ann
hunted near the pond in the
park.
They could hear a song there.
They saw a toad in the pond.
He was fat Father Toad.

Father Toad had a very good
    song.
It had a high sound
    like a high sweet whistle.
It had a soft low sound, too.
Father Toad did not open his
    mouth to sing high and low
    sounds.
But his throat was round
    like a little balloon.

Mother Toad was in the pond,
    too, but she had no song to
    sing.
She did not make her throat
    round like a little balloon.
She liked sweet songs in spring.
So she came near while
    Father Toad made high
    sounds and low sounds.

Mother Toad laid eggs in the
  pond.
She did not sit on her eggs.
Her body was cold and so she
  could not keep her eggs
  warm.
She went away from them.
The eggs were warm without
  her.
The sunshine made them warm.

Baby toads were in the eggs.
We call baby toads tadpoles.
They hatched in the warm
    sunshine.
They were not like grown toads.
The tadpoles had no legs at all
    but they had long tails.
They could swim with their
    tails.

The young tadpoles were
   hungry.

Father and Mother Toad did
   not hunt for their tadpoles.

The tadpoles hunted their own
   food.

They changed shape as they
   grew.

Their mouths were not so little
   and their tails were not so
   big.

The tadpoles all had legs
   when they grew old enough.
First each tadpole had two legs.
Then each of them had three
   legs.
After a while each one had
   four legs and no tail.

So the tadpoles changed to
   toads.
They were very little toads.
The body of each young toad
   was about half an inch long.

One day some rain wet the
   ground.
The little toads liked the rain.
They came out of the water
   and hopped on the ground.
After that they hunted on land.

Ted and Ann came out in the
rain.

They came to the park to play.

They hunted near the pond
and found the young toads.

They watched the little toads
while they hopped on the
ground.

Then Ted and Ann hopped,
too!

Pussy Willows

Ted and Ann hunted in the park
and found willows near the
pond.
The willows had many branches.
Willow flowers grew on the
branches.
But some were not like the
others.

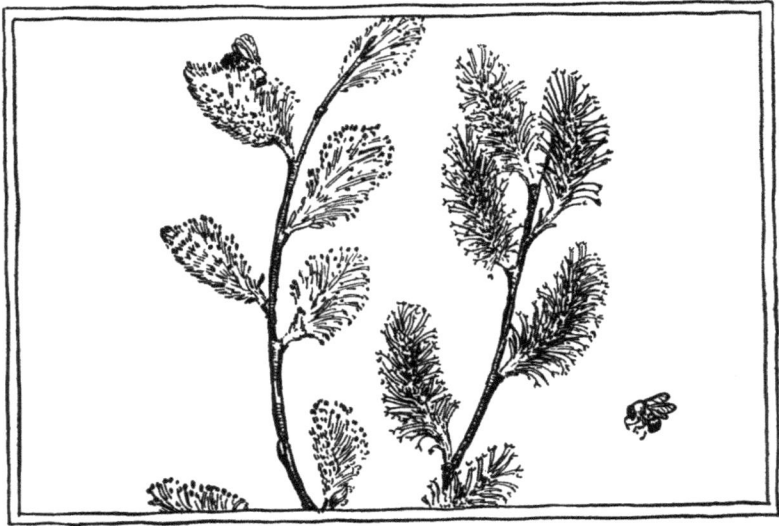

One willow had flowers with
  nectar and pollen but no
  seeds.
One willow had flowers with
  nectar and seeds but no
  pollen.
The baby seeds in the flowers
  could not live without pollen.
How did the seeds get some
  pollen?
Little bees took the pollen.

The bees did not know about
seeds.
They did not know that the
seeds could not live without
pollen.
The bees went to the willows for
food for baby bees.
They went for nectar and pollen.
Some pollen fell on them like
dust.
So they took it on their hairs
to the flowers without pollen.
Some fell from the hairs like
dust when they went there
for nectar.
That is how the young willow
seeds could have pollen
and live. The willows gave
the bees food and the bees
helped the willows.

One day Mr. Long told Ted and
Ann about willow flowers and
bees.

He said, "Bumblebees and honey
bees and other bees come to
willows. They come for nectar
and pollen. Honey bees make
very good honey from nectar
in willow flowers."

Ted and Ann liked honey to
eat.

They often came to the willows to watch the honey bees.

"The flowers are pretty," said Ann. "Some parts of them are yellow. Some parts are gray and as soft as the fur a pussy has."

Ted said, "Perhaps that is why people call them pussy willows."

Ann asked, "Are you glad bees find pollen on this bush and take it to that other willow? So that willow can have seeds!"

"Yes," said Ted, "I should say I am!"

Robins

Father Robin lived in the park
and so did Mother Robin.
Father Robin liked to sing in
spring.
Mother Robin liked to hear him
sing.
His spring song had a happy
sound.

Father Robin had a black
head with a little white
near his eyes.
His throat was white and
black and his bill was
yellow.
He had a gray back and red
front.
Mother Robin looked very
much like Father Robin.

Mother Robin hunted in a tree
and found a good branch.
Then she made a nest on the
branch.
She made it with mud and old
grass.
She could use mud while it was
wet.
So she made the mud nest
a good shape to sit in.
She put in some dry brown
grass.
Then it was a soft nest for eggs.

Mother Robin laid one egg each
day for four days.
So she had four eggs in her
nest.
She sat on them and kept them
warm.

Father Robin hunted for food and
  gave Mother Robin some of it.

Ted and Ann found the nest
  and asked Mr. Long about it.

Mr. Long held Ann up to the
  nest so she could see the eggs.
"What pretty blue eggs!" said Ann.

Then Mr. Long held Ted up to
  see.
"What pretty green eggs!" Ted
  said.

Ann and Ted and Mr. Long
  laughed.
"Are the eggs blue?" asked Ted.
"Are they green?" asked Ann.

"It is hard to tell," said Mr. Long,
  "but most people call them
  blue."

Ted and Ann often came to
the park to see Mother and
Father Robin.

They were quiet when they
came and did not scare the
birds.

One day they saw four young
robins that could hop on the
ground.

They were too young to fly.

A Brown Cocoon

Ted and Ann hunted in the
park and found a brown
cocoon.

The brown cocoon was on a
branch.

It had been there all winter.

Ted and Ann found it one spring
day.

A caterpillar made the cocoon.
It made the cocoon with silk.
The caterpillar had some glands
  in its body.
The silk came from the glands.
The silk came out of a hole
  near the mouth of the
  caterpillar.

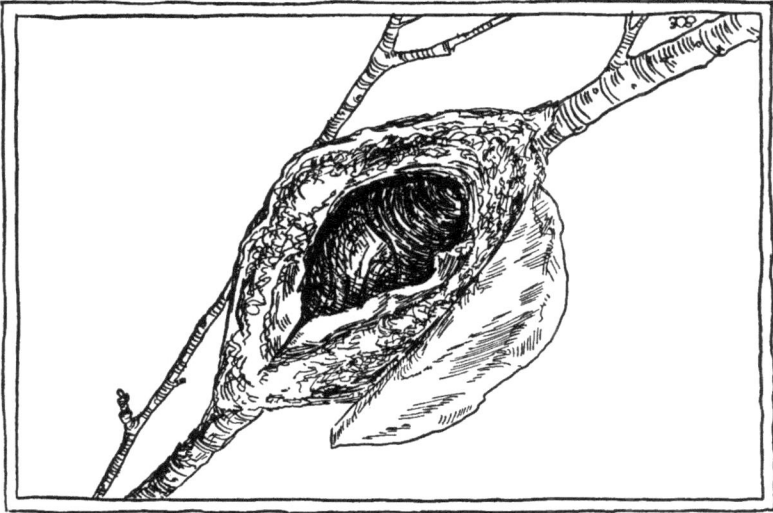

The caterpillar made the cocoon
all around its body.
Then the caterpillar changed
into a brown pupa.
The pupa had no mouth or
legs.
The pupa could not eat or
creep.
It rested in the cocoon all
winter.

Ted and Ann found the cocoon and Mr. Long told them about it.

"A big green caterpillar made that cocoon," he said.
"It had sharp spines on its body. They were red, blue, and yellow."

"It had pretty colors!" said Ann.

"Where did it come from?" said Ted.

"A moth laid an egg," said Mr. Long, "with a baby caterpillar in it. The caterpillar hatched and grew. Then it made a silk cocoon and changed into a brown pupa. Some day it will be a pretty moth."

"May we have the cocoon?" asked Ted.

Mr. Long gave them the cocoon, and they took it to Miss Bell.

She showed it to the girls and boys.

"What is in it?" asked a boy.

"A pupa is in it," said Miss Bell. "A moth laid an egg.
A caterpillar hatched from the egg.
It ate and grew and made a cocoon.
Then it changed to a pupa."

"What will the pupa change to?" asked one of the girls.

"Wait and see!" said Miss Bell.

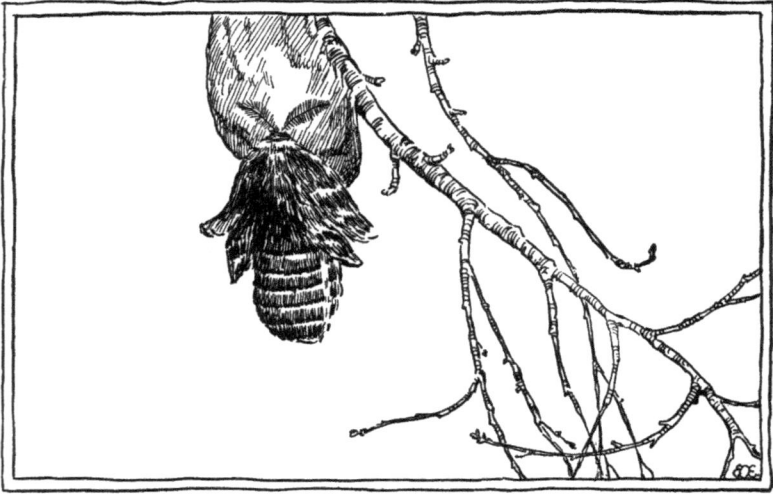

One day Miss Bell said,
   "I hear a sound in the
   cocoon."

The boys and girls all watched
   it.

A moth came out of the
   cocoon.
It had two feelers on its head.
The feelers looked like feathers.

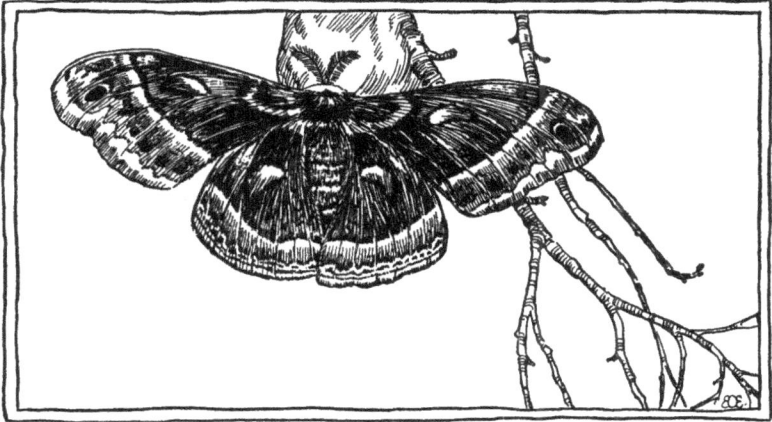

The moth had four wings.
At first the wings were little.
The boys and girls
    watched them grow.
The wings were light and dark
    brown with red and white on
    them.
There were two black spots
    with some pretty blue on
    them.

Miss Bell said,
   "If we keep the moth in
   school it will fly to the
   window and break its wings."

"Will it fly to-day?" asked Ann.

"No," said Miss Bell, "it will
   wait and fly in the night."

"I will take it outdoors," said
   Ted, "and put it on a tree."

Then Ted put the moth on a
   branch.
It rested there all that day.
The moth waked when night
   came.
It liked the dark night.
So the moth flew away in the
   dark.

Acorns

An old oak tree lived in the
  park.
Many acorns grew on the oak
  tree.
The acorns were seeds of the
  oak.
They had hard brown shells.
A baby oak tree was in each
  shell.

Some squirrels hunted for acorns.
They liked acorns to eat.
They put acorns in holes in
    trees.
They put acorns in the ground,
    too.
They dug up some when winter
    came.
But some they left in the
    ground and did not find all
    winter.

The ground was warm in spring
and rain wet the acorn shells.

In spring the baby oak trees
grew too big for their shells.
The hard brown acorn shells
broke and the little trees
sprouted.

Ted and Ann hunted in the park
and found many young oaks.
Then they went to tell Mr. Long.

"Mr. Long, please come to see
how the acorns grew!" said
Ann.

Mr. Long went with Ted and
Ann.
He looked at the young trees.
He said, "The trees are too
thick."

Mr. Long said, "You may have
all the young oaks you will
dig."

Ted and Ann dug some little
trees and put them in a box.

"Mr. Long, we thank you for so
many young oak trees," they
said.

Ted and Ann showed their young oaks to Uncle Jim.

"Wet the roots," said Uncle Jim. "We will plant them Saturday."

On Saturday their uncle said, "Take your trees to my car, and we will go to the old farm."

So they all went to the farm where Uncle Jim had lived when he was a boy as young as Ted.

Uncle Jim showed Ted and Ann where to plant their trees. There was a good place for them to grow, near a wall.

Ted and Ann were very happy
about their little oak trees.

"When they grow old enough
they will have acorns," said
Ann.

"Perhaps some squirrels will
hunt and find the acorns,"
said Ted.

"Yes," said Ann, "and perhaps
they will put some in the
wall and eat them in winter."

"Perhaps they will put some
in the ground, too!" said Ted.
"Some acorns may grow
and then there will be more
oak trees on the farm."

"I hope we may see these trees
when they have acorns," said
Ann.

"We shall be grown," said Ted,
"when these oaks have acorns.
Perhaps we shall be as old
as Uncle and Mother and
Father!"

Swans

Two white swans lived in the
  park.
They were Father and Mother
  Swan.
Their bodies were a little
    like boats and their feet
    were a little like paddles.

Ted and Ann often came to see
the swans swim in the pond.

"They move in the water like
boats," said Ted, "with feet
for paddles."

"What long necks they have
and how they bend them!"
said Ann.

One day there were
    six gray swans near the two
    white swans.

"Mr. Long," said Ann,
    "will you please tell us about
    the six gray swans?"

Mr. Long told them,
    "Mother Swan laid some eggs.
    These birds came from her
    eggs."

"Will their gray feathers fall out
    and new feathers grow?" said
    Ann.

"Yes," said Mr. Long, "and then
    the six young swans will be
    white like their father and
    mother."

A Water Lily

When warm summer came, Ted
and Ann hunted for summer
flowers.
One day they found a water
lily in the pond in the park.
It was white and green and
yellow.

The outside of the lily was green.
The middle parts were yellow.
All the other parts were white.

Many bees came to get lily
    pollen. They took some to their
    young bees.
Flies often came to eat pollen
    for their own food.
They did not take it to young
    flies.
One day Mr. Long told Ted and
    Ann about the bees and flies.

"Each bee has four wings," he
    said, "and each fly has two
    wings."

So Ted and Ann looked at the
    wings of the bees and the
    flies.

An Animal with Eight Legs

Ted and Ann went to see Mr. Long.

He said, "To-day I saw an animal. What do you think it was?"

So they asked about the animal.

"It has no fur," said Mr. Long.

"Then it was not a mole," said Ann, "or a squirrel or a woodchuck."

"It had no feathers," said Mr. Long.

"Then it was not a robin," said Ted, "or a bluebird or a woodpecker or a hummingbird or a swallow or any other kind of bird."

"Did it have six legs?" asked Ann.

"It had more than six," he said.

"Then it was not an ant," said Ann, "or any other grown insect. All grown insects have six legs."

"It made silk," said Mr. Long.

"Caterpillars make silk," said Ted.

"The animal I saw," said Mr. Long, "was not a caterpillar."

"How many legs did the animal have?" asked Ann.

"It had eight legs," said Mr. Long.

"Will you please tell us what animal has eight legs?" asked Ann.

Mr. Long smiled and said, "No, I will not tell you what it is."

So they hunted in the park to find an animal that had eight legs!

Ted and Ann found a little
   animal without feathers or
   fur.
It was on a pretty silk web.
Its back was brown and
   yellow.
It had eight eyes and eight
   legs.
The animal on the silk web
   was a spider.

The spider had glands in her
   body.
Some of them were silk glands.

Silk came out of the silk glands
   when the spider needed it.
The silk was like very fine
   thread.

The spider made a web with
   silk. The web was her home
   in summer.
It was a good home for her.

Some flies came to her web
   and they could not get away.
They could not walk on the silk.

The spider could walk on her
   web.
She took the flies and ate them.
The flies were good food for her.

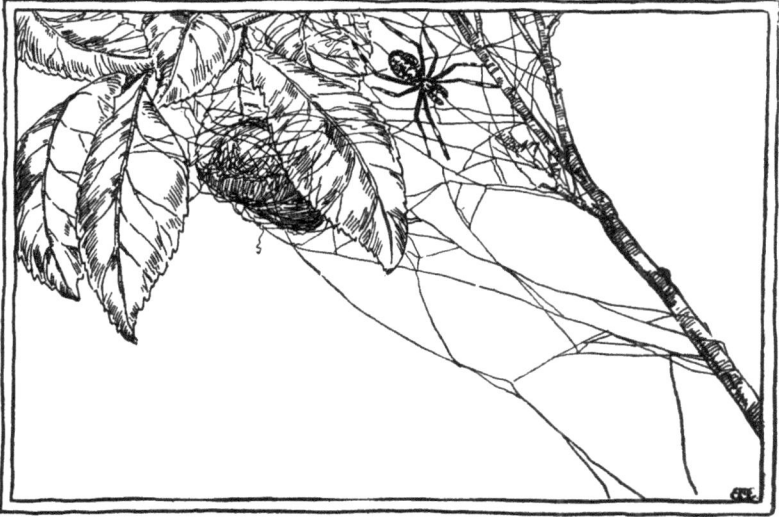

The spider laid eggs in the fall.
She did not lay them in her
    web.
She put some soft white silk
    around her eggs for a nest.
This nest was round like a ball.
Baby spiders hatched in the
    nest.
Some day they would make
    webs, too.

Can You Tell?

Did Mother Toad warm her eggs or did the sun keep them warm?

Do ants and bees have six legs or do they have eight legs?

Do acorns grow on oak trees or do they grow on willow trees?

Do old swans have gray feathers and are young swans white?

Was the cocoon made by a moth or was it made by a caterpillar or was it made by a pupa?

What Was It?

It had eight legs.
It made a silk web.
It liked to eat flies.
What was it?

It grew in a pond.
It was white and green and
  yellow.
Bees came to it for pollen.
What was it?

It rested all day.
It waked when night came.
It flew away in the dark.
What was it?

The Park Is a Happy Place To Be

The park is a happy place to be,
There are so many things to see!

I like the pond in early spring,
For then the frogs begin to sing.

In summer time I like the
  breeze
And humming sounds of little
  bees.

In fall the squirrels hunt and
  play
And hide their many nuts away.

When winter comes the park is
  white,
And sunshine seems so very
  bright!

PART FOUR

Hunting in the Zoo

Father's Game

Ted and Ann often talked with
their father and mother about
hunting.
They told them about all the
games they liked to play with
Uncle Jim and Miss Bell and
Mr. Long.

One day their father said to
them, "You are very good
hunters. You find bees and birds
and toads and little animals
with fur. You are quiet and
watch to see how they look
and what they do.

"You help take care of plants and
watch to see their flowers grow.
You do not often break the
stems, but leave the flowers
for other boys and girls to see
and like."

Then Father smiled and asked
them, "Will you come to hunt
with me? I know a good
hunting game. I call it Hunting
in the Zoo."

The Zoo

Part of the zoo was like a park.
There were many ponds in the
park. Big pink birds waded in
one pond. There were trees
in the zoo and some deer ran
near the trees.

There were big stones in the
zoo and some bears climbed
the stones.

"May we see the bears?" asked
Ted.

"May we see the deer?" asked
Ann.

Father smiled and looked at
Ted. "Ann may choose first,"
said Ted.

So they all went to watch the
deer.

Eleanor Osborn Eadie

Deer with White Tails

"See their white tails!" said Ann.

"Are all deer like these?"
    asked Ted.

"No," said their father,
    "there are different kinds.
    Some do not have white
    tails."

Father White Tails have horns.
Their horns are not like the
    horns that a cow has.

A deer has horns with branches.
A cow has horns without
    branches.

The horns of white-tail deer
    fall off their heads each year.
Then new horns grow on their
    heads.

If people cut the horns off a
    cow, new horns do not grow.

Ted and Ann looked at the
    horns on the heads of the
    father deer.
They asked Father about the
    horns that deer and cows
    have.

"See that little deer!" said Ann.

"It has white spots," said Ted.

"It is a baby deer," said Father. "Its first hair will fall out. New brown hair will grow and then the young deer will have no spots."

"Do baby cows have spots?" said Ted.

"They have no spots like these, but their first hair falls out and new hair grows," said Father.

"Do the old deer and the old cows have new hair, too?" asked Ted.

"Yes," said Father, "old cows and old deer have new hair each year."

Then Ted said, "Look at their feet! Deer have hoofs and so do cows."

"There are some other kinds of deer in this zoo," said Father.

So they went to see the other deer.

Bears

Father went with Ted and Ann to see all the bears in the zoo.

The bears lived in outdoor cages. The cages were kept clean for them. The cages were in the sunshine.

There were stones in the cages big enough for bears to climb.

There were holes near the stones big enough for bears to sleep in.
The holes were clean and dry.

The bears played in the sunshine and slept in the dark holes.

A brown bear was in one
cage.
She could walk on her two
hind feet.
The brown bear was very
tame and she liked to see
people.
Ted and Ann laughed to see
her walk on her two hind
feet.

There were six bears in one
    cage.
Their name was Black Bear.
Their fur was black and brown.
They could walk on all four feet.
They could walk on their hind
    feet.
There were old trees in their
    cage.
The black bears played and
    climbed.

Father said, "Once, I saw a bear climb an old tree on the farm. The tree had a big hole in it. The hole was filled with honey. Some bees had put it there. The bear put his paws in the hole and took out some of the honey. He liked to eat sweet food."

"Did the bees sting him?" asked Ted. "Did they scare the bear away?"

"The bees buzzed," said Father. "Their buzzing was a cross sound. But they could not hurt the bear. His fur was too thick for them. The bees could not scare the bear."

There were white bears in the
zoo.

They had a good pond in their
cage and there was ice in it.

The bears liked to swim in the
pond and put their paws on
the ice.

The zoo would be too warm for
them without the ice.

Raccoons

One day Father and Ted and
Ann went to the zoo to hunt
for raccoons.
They found two raccoons in a
tree.
The raccoons were quiet in
the tree.
They looked very sleepy.

After a while one of the
    raccoons climbed down a
    tree and Ted and Ann
    could see her face.

Part of her face was black
    and her eyes were in the
    black part.
The fur on other parts of her
    body had gray and brown
    and black and yellow hairs
    in it.

"It is hard to tell," said Ann,
    "what color a raccoon is!"

The raccoon did not walk
    on her toes as a cat walks.
She put her feet flat on the
    ground like a bear when it
    walks.

When the raccoons were
  hungry they put their food
  in water.
Then they took it out and ate
  it.

"I wish we had a raccoon!" said
  Ted.

Father smiled and told him,
  "Raccoons are often good
  pets."

An Animal with Spines

A boy came to the porcupine
cage. He opened the cage
and went in. The boy took
a box into the cage. It was
large enough for a porcupine.
The boy was Robert Brown.

Robert moved slowly in the
cage.

He did not scare the
porcupines.

"Spiny, Spiny, come to me," he
said, "and I will take you
home."

Spiny had a fat body and short
legs but he went as fast as
he could.

Spiny made a soft happy sound.

"You are glad I came!" said
    Robert.
Robert rubbed his pet slowly.
He rubbed Spiny from head to
    tail.
He did not rub from tail to
    head.

Robert opened his box and said,
    "Are you hungry, Spiny?
    There is good food in the
    box."

Spiny climbed into the box
    and ate some of the food.

Robert closed the box and took
    it out of the porcupine cage.
He saw Ted and Ann and
    smiled.

"Would you like to see my
    pet? It is a porcupine," said
    Robert.

"Yes, please, we should!" said
    Ted.

Ted and Ann looked at Spiny.
    They saw his black and gray
    hairs. Many of the hairs had
    white ends.

The porcupine had long sharp spines on his head and back and tail.

"Did your porcupine ever hurt you with his spines?" asked Ann.

"He would not hurt me," said Robert. "He would not hurt his friends."

"Would he hurt a dog?" asked Ted.

"He hurt a dog once," said Robert. "The dog ran after him. Spiny hit the dog with his tail. Then the dog had spines in his nose and they hurt. I asked a man to take them out. That dog did not chase Spiny again!"

"You were kind to show us Spiny and tell us about him," said Ted.

Then they all went home.

The Biggest Animal
in the Zoo

"An elephant is the biggest animal in the zoo," said Ted one day.

"I wish we could see one," said Ann.

So they went to the zoo with Father.
They saw an elephant.

The elephant had a big heavy
head.
Her head was too big and
heavy for a long neck to
hold up.
The elephant had a short neck.
She could not put her mouth
down to the ground to eat.
She could not eat as a cow can.

So how could she get food to
eat?

The elephant had a long nose.
Her nose was so long she could
put the end of it down to
the ground.
She could hold food with her
nose and put it into her
mouth.
So that is the way she ate!

Ted watched the elephant and said, "An elephant eats with her nose. Can she drink with her nose, too?"

"Watch her drink," said Father.

She put the end of her long nose into water and took some water up into the two holes in her nose.
Then she put the end of her nose into her mouth and the water went down her throat.

"How does she breathe?" asked Ann.

"As you do," said her father. "She takes air into two holes in her nose when she breathes."

"The long nose of an elephant
has a different name.
We call it a trunk," said
Father.

"Her two biggest teeth are not
like the teeth most animals
have. We call these big teeth
tusks."

"Shall we play a game," said
   Ted, "and tell how the
   elephant is different?"

"She has no horns on her head,"
   said Ann, "so she is different
   from the cows at the farm."

"Her hair is not fur," said Ted,
   "so she is different from a
   mole."

"Her tail is not so big as her
   nose," said Ann, "so she is
   different from a squirrel or a
   cat."

Father laughed and said,
   "She has five hoofs on each
   foot. So she is different from
   a deer."

Some Zoo Birds

One day Ted and Ann went to
  the zoo with their father to
  see the birds.
Many birds were in a big cage.
They flew about in the cage or
  sat in the branches of a
  tree.

There were swans in the zoo pond. Some were white and some were black.

"Are the black swans the young of the white swans?" asked Ted.

"Will their new feathers be white like the others?" asked Ann.

"No, the black swans are old birds," said Father, "and their new feathers will be black, too."

There were geese in the zoo pond.
The geese were much like swans but they were not so big and their necks were not so long.
Their flat feet were like paddles.

There were ducks in the zoo
pond.
The ducks were much like
geese but they were not so
big and their necks were not
so long.
Their flat feet were like paddles.

There were many kinds of
ducks with feathers of
different colors.

Some of the birds in the zoo
pond did not swim with
paddle feet.
They waded with very long
legs.

There were different kinds
of birds that waded in the
water.

Their bodies had different
shapes and different colors.
Some of them were pink and
white with red and black
feathers in their pretty wings.

"See this pink bird!" said Ann.
"It likes to bend its long
neck."

"It has a queer bill," said Ted.

A pink bird put its big bill
into the water and found
food.

"It is a flamingo," said Father.
"One kind of flamingo is red."

"I wish I could see one," said
Ann. So they hunted for a
red flamingo.

Which Is It?

Which animal has horns?
bear   deer   raccoon

Which bird swims in water?
robin   bluebird   swan

Which animal has feathers?
porcupine   bee   hummingbird

Which animal has four legs?
elephant   spider   woodpecker

Which plant has blue flowers?
dandelion forget-me-not water lily

Which animal has fur?
frog   mole   ant

Yes or No?

Do crickets have more wings
  than birds have?
Are insects and birds animals?
Do raccoons eat their food
  after they put it in water?
Do swans have feet shaped
  like the feet of robins?
Do insects have more feet
  than spiders have?
Do bank swallows dig holes
  with their feet?
Is the trunk of an elephant
  a long kind of mouth?